I0448103

GOING GREEN

The Most Comprehensive Guide To
Green Home Upgrades For All Budgets

By Jiles O'Neal

Copyright © 2016 by O'Neal Media Empire

onealmediaempire@gmail.com

Ordering Information:

Orders by U.S. trade bookstores and wholesalers. Please contact Amazon: **www.amazon.com**

Printed by Createspace

O'Neal Media Empire

Seattle, WA

ISBN-13: 978-1539482284

ISBN-10: 1539482286

First Edition

12 11 10 9 8 7 6 5 4 3 2 1

TABLE OF CONTENTS

HISTORY OF GOING GREEN

The most common definition of **"going green"** is: making more environmentally friendly decisions as to *reduce, reuse and recycle*.

Way back in 2500 BCE, the first war was fought over water. The war was fought between the kingdom of Lagesh and the kingdom of Umma in what is present day Iraq. Could this battle over a basic natural resource be the foundation of future environmentalism?[1]

World environmentalism began most recognizably in the Age of Enlightenment. This was a time in the 16-1700s where people were moving away from superstition, dogma and absolute monarchies. Ideas were increasingly based on science and reason, giving cause for people to start questioning authority. During this time forests and wooded areas began to be realized as important to the health of the planet and its inhabitants. Forests start getting protected from over building and protests take place by indigenous tribes to protect trees that they hold sacred. This era brought about a realization that clean water and a sewer system were important for public health. In 1721, Lady Mary Wortley Montagu, popularized the smallpox inoculation. In the 1760s, Benjamin Franklin attempted to regulate wastewater in Philadelphia; when he died in 1790, he left money to the city of Philadelphia to install pipes to bring fresh water into the city.

The first municipal sewer system was built in London in 1800 but the water system continued to be contaminated. In 1842, Edwin Chadwick authored a Report on Sanitary Conditions of the Laboring

Population of Great Britain. He advocated for public health reform so aggressively that the London Times wrote, "We prefer to take our chance of cholera than be bullied into public health."

The root of environmentalism in the United States can be traced back many centuries. In Henry David Thoreau's 1864 book "*The Maine Woods*", he called for federal preservation of untouched forests. Yosemite was made our first national park in 1872, the same year the Audubon Society was formed and the Sequoia and General Grant parks were established. John Muir was instrumental in getting Yosemite its national park status and founded the Sierra Club in 1892. After his death, the John Muir trail was completed on what would have been his 100th birthday. The popular trail passes through some of the most scenic areas of the Sierra mountains.

The mid 1800's was a time of nonstop discoveries in the field of environmental and public health. A cholera outbreak in Great Britain led to the formation of the Public Health Act, which was ultimately a failure. In 1954 a London doctor named John Snow realize that the spread of cholera was localized to part of the city that got their water from unfiltered sources. He shut off the water pump in that area and broke off the handle. The following years showed a sharp decline in cholera patients.

After the Civil War broke out in the United States, many environmental and health problems became apparent. The US Sanitary Commission was formed in 1861, the US Department of Agriculture and Homestead Act were created in 1862. The first mention of "Greenhouse Gasses" were used in a lecture by John Tyndall to the British Royal society.

In the early 1900's, President Theodore Roosevelt made conservation a top priority. He established many more national parks, forests and monuments in an effort to preserve the nation's resources. During this time there was a lot of concern about land and wilderness, but it wasn't until the 1948 disaster in Donora Pennsylvania (commonly referred to as the *Death Fog*), that people started to really take note of environmental conditions and how they affect people individually. Rachel Carson published the bestseller "*Silent Spring*" in 1962 which exposed the negative effects of pesticides on people and wildlife. A handful of other man made disasters started to bring the idea of environmentalism to the general population. The Wilderness Act was passed in 1964 and the Environmental Protection Agency was founded in 1970.

The end of the 20th century saw major events in the area of environmentalism. The toxic waste at The Love Canal in 1978, the nuclear meltdown at Three Mile Island Nuclear Generating Station in 1979 and the Exxon Valdez oil spill in 1989 took a massive toll on the environment and human health. The more people became aware of environmental concerns, the more people started to act to make change. The late 1900's gave us the clean air act, a ban on DDT insecticide, the national environmental policy act as well as many other legislations to control pollution.

The beginning of the 21st century has shown a lot of cooperation between nations to decrease global greenhouse emissions. A majority of the world's nations came together to ratify the Kyoto Treaty in

2005 which is an international treaty that commits various nations to lower greenhouse gasses. Just two years later, Billionaire Richard Branson offered a 25 million dollar prize for anybody who could develop a way to reduce greenhouse gases from Earth's atmosphere by one billion tons (900 million metric tons) per year. Throughout the last decade, innovations in alternative energy, such as solar power and wind energy, have taken off like a rocket. Advancements in electric cars, higher fuel efficiency, and energy saving home appliances have become major industries in many countries. The dedication of people who want to protect the planet and all the creatures that live here is off the charts.

All it takes is a little effort and some creativity and you too can go green and start helping save the planet we live on and the other animals we live with.

ENVIRONMENTAL TIMELINE

2500 BCE: First war over water Middle East.

80: Roman Senate passes a law to protect stored water in order to use it for sewer and street cleaning.

676: **Cuthbert of Lindisfarne** enacts protection legislation for birds on the **Farne Islands**.

1079: English King William (the Conqueror) establishes the ***New Forest*** as a hunting preserve.

1300s: France introduces the *Forest Code* aimed at regulation wood production by the Navy.

1347-1350s: *Bubonic plague* kills up to 75% of the populations of Europe and Asia, creating the laws regarding public health and quarantines.

1388: British Parliament passes an act forbidding the throwing of filth and garbage into ditches, rivers and waters. City of Cambridge also passes the first urban sanitary laws in England.

1516: Thomas Moore of England writes Utopia.

1661: John Evelyn writes "Fumifugium, or the Inconvenience of the Aer and Smoake of London Dissipated" to propose remedies for London's air pollution problem. These include large public parks and lots of flowers.

1669: Stricter forest codes introduced in France, again aimed at regulating wood production for the Navy.

1690: Colonial Governor William Penn requires Pennsylvania settlers to preserve one acre of trees for every five acres cleared.

1690s: Paris becomes first European city with extensive sewer system.

1721: Lady Mary Wortley Montagu, popularizes smallpox inoculation, a practice she had observed in Turkey.

1730: 294 men and 69 women of the **Bishnoi** branch of the Hindu faith were killed while hugging trees in protest of the trees being harvested. This gave us the term "treehugger".

1762 –1769: Philadelphia committee led by Benjamin Franklin attempts to regulate waste disposal and water pollution.

1790, April 17: Benjamin Franklin dies, leaving money in a widely publicized codicil to his will to build fresh water pipeline to Philadelphia due to the link between bad water and disease.

1800: Beginnings of first modern municipal sewers in London.

1805: Cousin de Grainville writes *The Last Man*, perhaps the first doomsday tale. The French author describes the human race dwindling through natural processes to a lonely end. De Grainville committed suicide shortly after the novel was published.

1822: First British humane law, with laws prohibiting dogfighting and cockfighting following in 1835. Rat-fighting was not banned until 1911.

1832: Arkansas Hot Springs established as a national reservation, setting a precedent for Yellowstone and eventually, a national park system

1842: Edwin Chadwick writes The Sanitary Condition of the Labouring Population of Great Britain. Report is first scientific inquiry linking high rates of infectious disease and child mortality to grossly unsanitary conditions and polluted drinking water. For every person who died of old age or violence in Britain in the year 1839, the commission reports, eight died of infectious disease.

1847: **Gas-works Clauses Act 1847** passed by Parliament. One of the first attempts to regulate the environmental impacts of industry, the act prohibited discharge of coal tar and other byproducts of manufactured gas works into streams and rivers..

1848: May 7, Public Health Act is passed by a reluctant Parliament fearful of spread of cholera. National Board of Health is formed and leads local boards to regulate water supply, sewerage, offensive trades. Smoke abatement becomes a political responsibility of the health department. The board is a political failure, however.

1854: September 7 — John Snow (1813-1858), a London doctor, convinces local authorities to let him close down the water pump on Broad Street. After getting permission, he breaks the pump handle. The spread of cholera is slowed dramatically as a result

1855: First comprehensive city sewer plan in U.S. in Chicago. By 1905, all U.S. towns with population over 4,000 have city sewers. The Baltimore city sewer system, begun in 1915, is the last to be built.

1861: U.S. Sanitary Commission is formed to help relief efforts for Civil War soldiers.

1862: US Dept. of Agriculture established.

1862: Homestead Act passed in the US, encouraging settlement of the west.

1863: John Tyndall explains the "greenhouse effect" in a lecture to the British Royal Society entitled "On Radiation Through the Earth's Atmosphere."

1867: Wilderness advocate John Muir begins his **Thousand Mile Walk to the Gulf.**

1871: US Weather Bureau and U.S. Bureau of Commercial Fisheries join to become the National Oceanic and Atmospheric Administration (NOAA).

1875: American Forests founded by John Aston Warde to protect forests from unnecessary waste. The organization is probably the oldest US conservation group still in operation.

1885: U.S. Biological Survey created, partly out of concern over the near extermination of the buffalo and the passenger pigeon.

1887: Rio de Janeiro — First hemispheric health conference of a series that led to the Pan American Sanitary Bureau which later became the Pan American Health Organization, a regional arm of WHO.

1890, Sept. 25: Sequoia National Park established; Oct. 1 — Yosemite and General Grant National Parks established; all after authorization by Congress.

1892, May 28: **Sierra Club** founded by John Muir, Robert Underwood Johnson and William Colby "to do something for the wilderness and make the mountains glad."

1898: Coal Smoke Abatement Society formed to pressure government agencies to enforce pollution laws in England.

April 15, 1990: **Rudolph Diesel** demonstrates his compression-ignition engine and shows it can run on vegetable oil, which means that even if petroleum were to run out, industry would still have fuel;

1902: Congress passed a bill establishing Crater Lake National Park in Oregon.

1904: Two American engineers, H.E. Willsie and John Boyle, set up the Willsie Sun Co. in St. Louis in 1904. A solar power plant using ammonia drove a six horsepower engine

1905: **National Audubon Society** organized by George Bird Grinell to promote wildlife conservation.

1908, Jan. 9: President Roosevelt sets aside **Muir Woods** in California as a national park.

1909: France, Belgium and Austria ban white-lead interior paint.

1912: Frank Shuman's Sun Power Co. builds a massive solar irrigation pump in the Egyptian desert for the British government

1916: National Park Service created. President Woodrow Wilson created the national park system with the Organic Act of 1916 designed to "conserve the scenery and the natural and historic objects [and] leave them unimpaired for the enjoyment of future generations."

1922: League of Nations bans white-lead interior paint but the US declines to adopt the ban.

1926: First large scale survey of air pollution in U.S., in Salt Lake City.

1933, Nov 11: **First of the Dust Bowl storms** begin in the Midwest.

1935: Wilderness Society co-founded by Aldo Leopold and Arthur Carhardt.

1937: The term "greenhouse effect" is coined by Glen Thomas Trewartha, an assistant professor of geography at the University of Wisconsin, in his book An Introduction to Weather and Climate.

1941: Between 25,000 and 60,000 rooftop solar water heaters are being used, mostly in Florida and

California. In Miami 80 percent of new homes are built with solar hot water. War materials needs prevent industry expansion.

1947: Los Angeles Air Pollution Control District is the first air pollution control bureau in the nation.

1949: First US conference on air pollution sponsored by Public Health Service.

1955: Sept. 19 — Japan Council Against Atomic and Hydrogen Bombs (Gensuikyo) founded

1956, March 31: World's **first commercial nuclear electric power plant** is opened at Sellafield in the United Kingdom.

1959: California becomes first to impose automotive emissions standards, requiring "blow-by" valve to recycle crankcase emissions back through the carburetor.

June 8, 1960: US president Eisenhower signs a bill starting a two-year Public Health Service study into on air pollution from cars.

June 22, 1962: Silent Spring by Rachel Carson, first published in the New Yorker.

1965: Congress passes Water Quality Act setting standards for states, along with the Noise Control Act and Solid Waste Disposal Act.

1967: US Congress passes Air Quality Act / Clean Air Act which authorizes planning grants to state air pollution control agencies.

1967: Greenpeace is founded in Vancouver, Canada as the Don't Make A Wave Committee, a Quaker peace group, which becomes Greenpeace in 1971 after several years of disrupting nuclear tests in the South Pacific.

1970, March 21: **Earth Day** celebration in San Francisco, organized by John McConnell.

1970, July 9: Environmental Protection Agency proposed by President Richard Nixon

1972, December 31: Nationwide **ban on the pesticide DDT** takes effect.

1978: Lois Gibbs and her neighbors form the Love Canal Homeowners Association after finding that they were living on a major toxic waste dump in Niagara Falls, New York. According to her 1990 Goldman Award citation, Gibbs wondered if the neighborhood children's unusual health problems were connected to their exposure to leaking chemical waste owned by the Hooker Chemicals and Plastics Corp. which had used Love Canal as a toxic dump site in the 1940s and 1950s

1979: **Earth First!** organized by Dave Foreman, Howie Wolke and Mike Roselle.

1985: British scientist Joe Farman publishes discovery of ozone hole over Antarctica, confirmed by US NASA satellite monitoring

1989, March 3: European nations begin ban on ozone – depleting chemicals.

1993: President Clinton signs order restricting logging in old growth forests.

1997, Dec. 10: **Julia Butterfly Hill** climbs a 180 foot California Coast Redwood tree in defiance of loggers. She spends two years in the tree as a protest against redwood logging.

1999: Firefly Brigade starts in Manilla to promote bike riding and healthy urban living. The idea for the name has to do with the declining frequency of fireflies in urban settings.

2000, August: Rain forest logging banned in New Zealand following a 30 year campaign by environmental groups.

2001, July 22: G8 Summit in Genoa, Italy sees massive protests over the lack of environmental and labor standards in the push for international free trade

2002, August - September: **World Summit on Sustainable Development** (also known as Rio + 10), gathers in Johannesburg, South Africa.

2003, Dec 25: Twelve Eastern states win federal court injunction preventing Bush Administration from weakening clean air laws.

2005, Feb 16: With a majority of the world's nations ratifying, the Kyoto Protocol officially goes into force without the U.S.

2006, June: Former U.S. vice president Al Gore releases **An Inconvenient Truth,** a documentary that describes global warming.

2007, Jan 10: European Union agrees to cut C02 emissions by 20% by 2020, compared to 1990 levels. Under the Kyoto protocol, the EU was already committed to an 8% decrease. The plan also called for biofuels to make up at least 10% of vehicle fuel by 2020

2007, Feb 9: Billionaire businessman and philanthropist Richard Branson of Britain sets a $25 million prize for anyone able to devise a way to reduce the amount of so-called greenhouse gases from the Earth's atmosphere by one billion tons (900 million metric tons) per year.

2008, May 13: Brazil's Environment Minister Marina Silva resigns to protest the failure to protect the Amazon rain forest

2008, July 9: Group of Eight (G-8) industrialized nations will cut greenhouse gas emissions in half by 2050, they agree. This is the first time that all eight countries made the climate commitment.

2009, Mar 30: President Obama signs the largest wilderness protection bill in 15 years, protecting two million acres in nine states.

2009 July 9: The Group of Eight (G-8) industrialized nations (U.S., Britain, Germany, France, Italy, Russia, Japan and Canada_ agree to reduce their greenhouse gas emissions by 80% by 2050, leading to hopes for a successful summit in Copenhagen, Denmark.

2009 Sept 30: US EPA announces new Clean Air Act regulations to reduce greenhouse gas emissions from electric power plants.

2010, January 1 — France sets a carbon tax of 17 Euros per ton on all fossil fuels, following similar but much higher taxes in Sweden (imposed as early as 1991), Denmark, Finland, Norway and Switzerland.

2010, April 28 — US Secretary of Interior Ken Salizar announces approval of controversial **Cape Wind** offshore wind electric project.

2010, Oct. 13 — Canada puts bisphenol A (BPA) on the toxic substances list. BPA is a common additive in plastics.

2010, May — **Germany decides to phase out** nuclear power, while Switzerland said it would build **no new nuclear reactors**.

2012, January 18 — US President Barack Obama denies an application from a Canadian company for a permit to build and operate the controversial Keystone XL oil pipeline.

2012, Feb. 22 — United Nations renewable energy agency kicks off "sustainable energy for all" program in 2012. The program is particularly targeted to the developing world, where one person in five lacks access to modern electricity, and nearly three billion people rely on wood, coal, charcoal or animal waste for cooking and heating.

2012, Feb. 22 — United Nations renewable energy agency kicks off "sustainable energy for all" program in 2012. The program is particularly targeted to the developing world, where one person in five lacks access to modern electricity, and nearly three billion people rely on wood, coal, charcoal or animal waste for cooking and heating.

Summer 2013 — Violent crime is down worldwide, and the correspondence to the decline in blood lead levels from taking lead out of gasoline is rather more than coincidental.

2014, Feb 16 – American science educator and engineer **Bill Nye** debates global warming with congresswoman Marsha Blackburn (R-TN).

2014, June 5 — Mountaintop Removal Mining — a scourge of Appalachia's environment — is one step closer to ending **after a federal district court ruling** that the practice is ruining water and aquatic ecosystems.

2015, July25 — Germany generates 78 percent of its electricity from wind and solar on this day, setting a new record.

2015, Nov 30 – Dec 12 — **United Nations Climate Change conference** (COP 21) — For the first time, all 195 UN member states agree on an "ambitious and balanced" plan to control climate change.

HOW TO USE THIS BOOK

This is intended to be the most comprehensive guide you will find on how to go green. It is broken down into four monetary categories.

- **Going Green Without Spending a Dime** = Free options.
- **Going Green For Next to Nothing** = Cheap, generally less than $100.
- **Going Green Within a Moderate Price Range** = Generally under $1000.
- **Going Green With a Pricetag** = Major upgrades, in the thousands of dollars.

Some of the option will show up in more than one monetary category. For example, **Going Green Without Spending a Dime** has the suggestion: *bike to work*. You may already own a bike and gear in order to do this, so no additional cost is required to implement this option. It is also included in the **Going Green WIthin a Moderate Price Range** category because you might need to buy a bicycle and gear in order to start biking to work. This could easily cost more than a few hundred dollars.

Within each monetary category, the options are broken down by where they would be implemented.

- **Around the House**
- **In the Car**
- **On the Go**
- **At Work**
- **Communication**

Keep in mind that some of these suggestions won't work for everyone. If you live in an apartment, condo or even own your own home in a development with a homeowner's association, installing solar panels or a wind turbine probably won't be in the cards. Also, a lot of suggestions in the **At Work** category might only work if you have a position in management or even own the building where your work is located.

There are many items that can crossover into multiple areas. For example, *use the stairs* is in the **On the Go** Category but could easily go in the **At Work** category. So at the end of every option description, any other areas where that option can be utilized will be in parenthesis. Example:

Use the stairs: Any time you visit a building with more than one floor, it's definitely tempting to jump on the elevator and have a machine lift you up a few levels to your desired destination. If you are going to the 68th floor of a downtown highrise, you can definitely justify the elevator ride. If you are going up to the 3rd or 4th floor on the other hand, there's no reason to not take the stairs. Not only do you save a little bit of energy, you get exercise. Even the most fit people on earth need daily exercise, so save a bit of energy and keep those lungs healthy. (At Work)

GOING GREEN WITHOUT SPENDING A DIME

Around The House

Recycle: This might seem obvious, but there are some people who don't know how to recycle. Not to mention the people who do recycle, but don't realize how much more that can be recycled. Most cities have recycling pick up that takes plastic, glass and cardboard. You can also recycle car batteries, cell phone batteries, regular batteries, printer ink cartridges, CD and DVD cases, televisions, CFL bulbs, and charging cables. Not every city accepts all of these items. Some municipal facilities don't take CD or DVD cases with the regular recycling and usually batteries, charging cables, televisions and CFL bulbs have to be dropped off at a specific location. Visit **www.earth911.com** to find out how where to take any recycleable in your home. Don't forget that you can recycle books you are done with by dropping them off at the library or by making a few bucks by selling them to a used book store. (At Work)

Upcycle old items and clothes: It's great to try to recycle anything you don't need anymore, but it's even better to upcycle it into something you can use. Not only are you not putting something into the garbage, but you're making something you need that you now don't have to go out and buy. Using old wire and turning it into jewelry. Taking old t-shirts and turning them into a scarf or a handbag. Taking old milk jugs and turning them into mini greenhouses for your garden. If you put your imagination to work, there are millions of things you can do to make old items serve a purpose again. When you run out of ideas, the internet is right there to give you a few million more.

Donate old items: Some people don't think about what is going into the garbage. They just toss unwanted items in the can and forget about it. Before you toss something away, take a look at it and consider whether or not it may be donated. Old electronics, toys, or kitchen devices may not be in perfect condition, but places like Goodwill and The Salvation Army will gladly accept them and resell them to people in need. If the item is no longer in working condition, donate it to a repair shop that can fix it and sell it. You can also put a lot of items that may be broken but still have some value on the curb and put a post on Craigslist letting people know it's free. Someone will come pick it up and it won't go in the landfill.

Donate wire hangers to dry cleaners: Some people don't know what to do with all of the wire hangers they have. In some areas, wire hangers can be recycled with your normal recycling, but it's not that common. One thing you can do, is donate them to a local dry cleaner. They won't have to buy more hangers and you won't have to put them in the trash. It's a win-win. Just put them in your car the next time you are running errands and drop them off at the closest dry cleaner.

Start a compost pile: There are so many things that go into our garbage cans that don't need to go there. Most food waste can go into the compost pile. Vegetables, fruits, rice, bread, expired boxed foods, egg shells and corn cobs/husks are just a few of the food items you can compost. You can also compost your used coffee grounds if you aren't using them as fertilizer for your garden. You don't want to put any meats or dairy in the compost bin as they will attract rodents, maggots and cause foul odors. You can also compost leaves, grass, paper, cardboard and dryer lint. If you want a full list of things that can and can't be composted at **www.getcomposting.com**.

Turn off the computer at the end of the day: It's impractical to turn your computer off every time you aren't going to be using it for a short amount of time. Even going out for an hour to run errands or get a bite to eat doesn't have to justify completely shutting down your system. It does make sense to do it at the end of the day though. When you know you are done on your computer for the day, shut it down and save a possible 10 - 16 hours of electricity. Even when your computer is asleep, it is still drawing power. (At Work)

Unplug electronics when done charging: This is something that I think everyone forgets about. Check on your electronics and unplug them when their battery is full. Cell phones, tablets, and handheld video game systems can all continue sucking electricity after the battery is full. These days it's not uncommon to have half a dozen electronic devices plugged in all day even though their batteries are full. A tip for making this an easy task: setup a power strip and charge your devices all in one place. Once all of the devices are charged, just turn off the power strip and you won't have to keep constantly plugging and unplugging your charging cables. (At Work)

Replace screensaver with sleep: For all of the times when you aren't done on your computer, but you plan on taking a break, don't use a screensaver. Some screensavers that are animated can actually be resource heavy and use more electricity than others. No matter what type of screensaver it is, it will still require the screen to stay on, which will suck more electricity than if the screen were off. Set your computer to go to sleep instead. This will shut off the screen and keep the computer idling just enough to not need a full reboot when you return. (At Work)

Reduce screen time: If you spend a lot of time in front of a screen, whether that be a television, computer monitor, or tablet, try to reduce your screen time by an hour each day. Any time that you don't need to be in front of a screen for work can easily be cut down. Free up some time to do chores or read a book. If you are the type of person who turns the TV on and lets it run all day in the background, stop. Switching from a TV to a radio for background noise will save energy and make your TV last longer.

Cancel the newspaper: We live in an electronic age. We get most of our news from the internet and the paper newspaper is becoming obsolete. Instead of having someone toss a bundle of paper onto your property every day, log into the news agency's website and read your news there every day. If you like to be away from the computer while you read the news, there are many inexpensive devices that you can use to read the newspaper online. (At Work)

Stop paper bank statements: In that electronic age we talked about previously, we don't really need people to mail us as much stuff as they do. We can check our accounts and view our statements online. My bank used to send the exact same paper statement to both myself and my wife for all three accounts we had. We got six separate paper statements on the same day every month plus a statement for each of my two kids' savings accounts. It was A LOT of paper. Now that I switch to paperless statements, I get an email once a month with a link to a PDF file. (At Work)

Paperless billing: When you cancel your paper bank statements, go online and sign up for paperless billing at the same time. Instead of having your bills come to you in the mail, just get an email notification and pay the bill online. I mean, do you really wait for the bill to come in the mail anyway. Chances are, you already check your bills online already, so why not get rid of that wasteful paper bill all together. Save trees, save time and save money. (At Work)

Opt out of mailing lists: One thing that I know frustrates everyone who has a mailbox is when you open it up and see that it's jam packed with nothing but junk mail. Some of the biggest offender are the companies who offer you pre-approved credit cards. You can go online and opt out of these offers at **www.optoutprescreen.com**. You can also opt out of commercial advertising, catalogs and magazine offer by visiting **www.dmachoice.org**. (At Work)

Stop phonebook delivery: In this day and age, nobody I know uses a physical phonebook. If you need to find something, you search it on google or use one of the many directory apps you can get for your smartphone or tablet. Now, not everyone is going to be able to opt out of receiving a phonebook. Companies like Yellowpages have fought hard to stop the phonebook from being phased out because those companies make a lot of money by selling ads in those phonebooks. They are gradually getting fewer and fewer, but you can always try to get opted out of having a phonebook delivered by visiting **www.yellowpagesoptout.com**. If you are in a city that still has a prominent amount of phonebook deliveries, try calling your local representatives to voice your concern about the waste. 70% of Americans never touch the phonebook that gets delivered to them. (At Work)

Download software: One of the quickest ways to get software when you buy it online is to just download it immediately after purchase. You used to have to wait for a physical disc in the mail, but with download speeds being as high as they are these days, there is usually no problem with someone being able to download a couple of gigabytes in a short amount of time. This saves packaging that is just going to get thrown away or recycled. Not only that, but it saves gas if you plan on going to the store to pick up the software if you don't want to wait for it in the mail. Just download it and burn it to a disc yourself if you want a physical backup. (At Work)

Water conservation: There are so many things you can do to conserve water for free. The first thing you should do is contact your local municipal water company and inquire about any water conservation devices they have. Some water companies give away free items like low flow shower heads, sink aerators that reduce the amount of gallons per minute (GPM) the faucet pumps out, and a device you can install in your toilet tank which makes it fill up more efficiently after each flush. I got one of these kits from my water company and after installing all of the items, my water bill went down by at least 20%. Other things you can consider when it comes to water conservation is to take a shorter shower. Even reducing your daily shower by a few minutes can save over 1,500 gallons of water per year. The best way to keep track of your showers is to get a small waterproof timer to keep in the shower. Also, when doing laundry, ensure the machine is set on the proper load size. I used to be guilty of always keep the washing machine set on "large" even if the load was smaller. Ultimately, it is best to try to always wash full loads, but life happens and sometimes you need to get a smaller load done. If that's the case, don't forget to change the settings.

Turn off hot water heater when out of town: I can't tell you how many people go on vacation without turning their hot water heater off. There's no reason to keep a tank full of water hot for a week while you aren't even going to be there. It makes sense if you are going to have someone house sit, but if nobody will be there, open the breaker box and flip the switch that controls the power to your hot water heater. It's a simple step that will save you a few bucks on your electricity bill.

Turn down water heater: Hot water heaters are most commonly set at 140 degrees. This gives you extremely hot water and most people can't handle water that temperature hitting their skin. If you want to conserve a little bit of energy, turn temperature setting on your water heater to heat the water to 130 degrees. This will save you a little bit of energy as your water heater won't have to work to heat up the water as much. This water should still be hot enough to wash dishes whether or not you have a dishwasher. If you don't use extremely hot water during showers, you can even turn the setting down to 120 degrees if you want.

Turn off hot tub when not in use: If you own a hot tub, then you know that they can suck a huge amount of energy. It's normal to keep a hot tub on all of the time since it takes quite a while to fully heat the tub up from it being off. If there are going to be longer periods where you aren't using the hot tub, then turn it off and then set yourself an alarm to turn it back on when there will be enough time for it to heat back up. A prime example of this would be if you were to leave on vacation. Another good example is if you only use it on the weekends. No reason to keep a hot tub warm for nobody.

Don't rinse dishes: It used to be common to have to rinse off all of your dishes to a nearly spotless state before putting them into the dishwasher. Older dishwashers weren't able to handle any food particles on the dishes, so they needed to be clean prior to them being cleaned... If that makes any sense. Current dishwashers are more powerful and have grinders to chew up food and keep it from clogging up the drain. So if you have a more modern dishwasher, it can save a lot of water if you stop rinsing the dishes before putting them into it. If you have an older dishwasher, it may save water if you stop using it. Washing dishes under running water tends to waste more water than a standard dishwasher, but if you have a double sink, you can use one to wash and one to rinse and get your dishes done with a minimum amount of water used. Everybody's situation is different, so play around with various methods and see what works best for you. It can also help to replace your kitchen sink aerator with one that puts out less GPM.

Wash laundry in cold water: Not all of your clothes need to be washed with hot water. In fact, some protein based stains like blood or sweat can actually be set in with the use of hot water. "Technological advancements in machines and detergents have made cold water washing a highly effective method," says **Clothing Doctor Steve Boorstein**. You will use less electricity heating water which will help the environment and help your pocketbook.

Hang dry clothes: Instead of using electricity to power a clothing dryer, why not hang dry your clothes. If you live in a dryer area, drying clothes outside on a clothesline can really make your garment have a freshness that you can't get with a dryer. Not to mention is it completely free and just uses the energy from the sun. This might not be an option for people in apartments or people who live in areas where the weather doesn't permit line drying. If you plan on drying clothing inside, ensure that you do it in a well ventilated area. A bathroom or laundry room with an exhaust fan or window is the best. If you dry clothes inside your home in areas that are not properly ventilated, the clothing could add up to a third more moisture into the air according to a **study by the Mackintosh School of Architecture** in Glasgow. This can cause mold, mildew and numerous health hazards.

Let your hair air dry: I know some people don't like the feeling of having wet hair, but if you do a good enough job with a towel, it's not impossible to make it through the short time it takes for your hair to air dry. Like anything with a heating element, hair dryers suck a large amount of power just to get your hair dry a few minutes quicker. If you need to blow dry your hair so it will be dry in time for you to leave for work, shuffle your schedule around so you shower earlier and have time for your hair to dry naturally. If you use a blowdryer to style your hair, well then maybe you should realize that it's not the 70's and feathered hair is out. Maybe this is a good reason to update your hairstyle!

Make sure your appliances are working properly: Keeping appliances clean and in proper working order will save energy in the long run. When appliances are dirty or not functioning properly, it makes them work harder in order to do their job. One big offender is your refrigerator. The coils on the back of the fridge collect dust and dirt and it makes it harder for the fridge to cool itself. Pulling out the refrigerator and cleaning the coils will ensure it is working as efficiently as possible.

Grab a blanket: Sometimes you get a little chilly when you are lounging at home, binge watching Netflix. Instead of turning up the heater, a lot of times all you need is a blanket. Having a couple of good blankets in the living room can make great substitutions to turning up the heat. Sometimes, even throwing on a sweater or sweatshirt works just fine as well.

Turn down thermostat 3 degrees: Just reducing your thermostat by 3 degrees can save energy in the long run. Not only that, but your gas or electric bill will also be lower. If you keep your thermostat set at 75 degrees, change it to 72 degrees. You will save energy and if you seal around your doors and windows to stop drafts (which we will talk about in the next chapter) you will probably be able to set it lower and be just as warm. Another thing to think about is your refrigerator and freezer. The warmer you make your house, the more those appliances have to work to keep your food cold. (At Work)

Clean heater ducts: We've brought up the fact that devices use more energy when they have to work harder, well that's especially true when it comes to your furnace. If your heating ducts are clogged with dust and debris, the hot air won't make it to its destination as easily. This will cause you to turn up the heat to make up for the hot air that is getting trapped in the ducts. Pull the heater grates off and stick a vacuum tube down there to clean out any dust and debris that may be clogging your heating ducts. You can also do this at the air intake vent and don't forget to vacuum off the filter in the furnace just to make sure airflow is strong. Of course if the air filter is too dirty you'll need to replace it (which we will talk about in the next chapter).

Use blinds and curtains appropriately: Blinds and curtains are great for privacy, but they also serve a great purpose for when you want to block out the sun. Not only to cut down on glare, but to block sunlight from coming into your home in the summer, heating up your home. The use of blinds and curtains in tandem with a ceiling fan can significantly reduce the amount of time you use your air conditioner. At the same time, in the colder seasons, open your blinds or curtains to let the sunlight in to naturally heat your home. You can turn down the thermostat and use 100% natural solar power for heat in your home. (At Work)

Use both sides of paper: I know I used to be guilty of printing out a document and then tossing it when it turned out that it was not needed. I'm an avid note taker myself. If I don't make myself a note or write a to-do list, I'll definitely forget something. So, instead of tossing or even recycling paper with a blank side, cut them into quarters and use them to make notes, to do lists, grocery lists, phone messages, the possibilities are endless. Also, any time you get documents in the mail or junk mail that has paper with one blank side, use that as well. If you are printing documents, cut your paper usage in half by printing on both sides. Some printers have settings that will do this automatically. Some printers you will have to flip the paper and feed it into the printer manually, but remember, it really is a small amount of work to save a ton of paper. (At Work)

Reuse gift wrapping: I know that a lot of people think that reusing gift wrapping is tacky, but it isn't. Get over it and start saving wrapping paper so you can cut down on paper wastage. Holidays are supposed to be happy times with our families, but they've turned into excuses to be extremely wasteful. Cards and wrapping paper and product packaging all flying into the garbage with gluttonous abandon. There is more than enough wrapping paper that is usually in good shape after a holiday event that it can be saved and reused.

Switch to e-cards: The greeting card industry is a multibillion dollar industry that wants you to tell your loved ones how you feel by sending them a paper card in a paper envelope multiple times per year. Do you really need to destroy trees and create waste to say happy birthday? Of course not! There are multiple sites online that offer e-cards inexpensively or even free. Just pick a design, fill out the form and hit send. It's that easy. Your family and friends will get an electronic card right in their e-mail which they can read and toss in their email's trash bin. No trees used, no waste created.

Stop using disposable items: There are so many disposable items around our home that it's easy to forget about them. Some are a necessity like toilet paper, but other can be replaced with a reusable version. Disposable razors can be replaced with reusable razors. This way you only need to replace the blades. If you are really adventurous, you can switch to a straight razor that never needs to be replaced (more about razors in the Going Green For Next To Nothing section). If you use disposable toothpicks, you can get reusable toothpicks that not only reduce waste, but do a better job than standard wood toothpicks do. Disposable straws, utensils and plates can all be replaced with reusable versions. Honestly, if you are a grown adult and you use disposable plates and forks, it's time to join the real world and get some dishes for your home. At Work)

Eat less meat: As much as it pains me to say, being a huge lover of meat, eating at least one vegetarian dish a week can help reduce damage to the environment. Science does show that the raising of animals for food does use much more resources than harvesting plant crops for food. Reducing your meat consumption can help reduce the amount animals being raised for food and can reduce greenhouse gasses. If you love meat, just reducing one meal a week with a vegetarian option can add up to big savings in the environmental department.

Take off your shoes: One small habit you can adopt at home is to take off your shoes inside of your house. Most of the dirt in your home will be tracked in from the outside. You can reduce the amount of vacuuming you do if you just leave those filthy shoes by the door when you come in the house.

Mow the lawn less often: Lawns are such a big deal in the United States. I understand that you want your property to look nice, but people seem to be more concerned with their lawn than the planet. Running a lawn mower, a weed eater or constantly watering the grass to ensure that it stays green. If everyone would just let their grass grow out a little longer, we could save on powering up the garden machines.

Save coffee grounds to use as fertilizer. One major gardening tip is to put your used coffee grounds in your garden as fertilizer. One obvious way to use coffee grounds as fertilizer is to put them into your compost. Another way is to put them straight into the soil around your plants, which improves drainage, water retention and aerates the soil. One concern people have i the acidity in the coffee grounds negatively affecting the plants, but if you rinse the coffee grounds first, it will bring the pH down to a neutral level.

On The Go

Use your own coffee cup: If you're the type of person who stops in for a cup of black coffee every morning, you could be wasting a disposable cup every day when you can just bring your own. Bring your favorite mug or commuter cup to the coffee shop and have them fill that up. You will not only eliminate a ton of waste, you might actually charge less for not using one of their cups. (At Work)

Pre-plan errands: I used to go out three or four times during the weekend because I had errands to run and I didn't plan ahead. I would run out to the post office and stop at the grocery store. Then I would run back out to pick up prescriptions. Then I'd remember that I needed something from the hardware store and I'd run out again. I would waste a half a tank of gas in a weekend just by running around town sporadically. Instead, plan ahead, make a list and get all of your errands done in one trip. You can route your trip to hit everywhere you need to go in the shortest route possible. Saving gas, saving wear and tear on your car and saving time. (At Work)

Switch to public transportation: Depending on where you live, you could get everywhere you need to go by using public transportation. Usually more feasible in larger cities, public transportation can reduce exhaust emissions as well as reduce expenses. You can reduce your fuel bill, your car insurance, car maintenance cost or parking fees which are common in many downtown areas of major cities.

Walk or bike: Another great option if you live in an area close enough to your errands is to walk or ride your bike. Not only will you get some exercise, but you will cut down on the carbon emissions produced by your car.

Use the stairs: Any time you visit a building with more than one floor, it's definitely tempting to jump on the elevator and have a machine lift you up a few levels to your desired destination. If you are going to 68th floor of a downtown highrise, you can definitely justify the elevator ride. If you are going up to the 3rd or 4th floor on the other hand, there's no reason to not take the stairs. Not only do you save a little bit of energy, you get exercise. Even the most fit people on earth need daily exercise, so save a save a bit of energy and keep those lungs healthy. (At Work)

Get books from the library: I know many people who love the feel and smell of a brand new book, but printing books uses a lot of paper. There are over 4 billion new books printed every year even though some of those same books sit on library and used book store shelves. Got a book you want to read? Stop by the used bookstore. Why not take a nice bike ride to the library? If they don't have what you want, put it on hold and grab something else to tide you over. There's no reason you need a brand new book.

Buy local / farmers market: I know that goods are cheap at the big box chain store, but those goods are flown, shipped, and trucked all over kingdom come before they actually make it to the shelves of your local super center. The amount of fuel used to truck goods across the country alone is as much as the citizens use in UK and Australia combined. Buying locally made or grown products can help reduce the amount of fuel used to ship goods around the country.

Buy from bulk foods: Not all grocery stores have a bulk section, but if there is one in your area, use it and cut down on waste and save money. Some grocery items come heavily packaged and buying those items in bulk can cut down on that packaging. You can also buy larger quantities without having to increase packaging. If that isn't incentive enough, I've found that the bulk food prices tend to be better than the pre-packaged food prices.

Don't take a receipt if you don't need it: A lot of registers require the cashier to hit a button in order to print out a receipt. I've noticed that in my area, people generally ask if you want a receipt before hitting that button. If you say 'no', they save paper and don't print a receipt. It also saves them time by not needing to change the printer roll as often. If you grab a soda and a candy bar, do you really need a receipt? Who are you going to need to prove that purchase to?

At Work

Telecommute: In this modern age, more and more work is being done on computers, over the Internet. The possibilities of doing work from home is becoming increasingly more common. If you have a home computer with Internet and a phone, it's likely that you can do all of your work tasks from your home office. Even if you can't telecommute every day, eliminating one or two trips to the office per week can save some carbon emissions depending on how far you commute and what area you live in. If you live in a cold area where you would need to heat your home all day when you would normally turn the heat down and go to work, it can actually be counterproductive. Especially if you don't commute very far. So check the numbers and cut out a few commutes per week if it will save some emissions.

Carpool: A great option if you live near coworkers is to carpool. In America, only about 10% of people carpool to work, which is a shame. Not only can you slash your carbon emissions and save gas, but you can also use the carpool lane which could save you some serious time. Post a message at work or send out an email asking if anyone would be interested in carpooling and
start saving time, money and the environment.

Bike to work: If you own a bicycle, you can start riding to work instead of driving your car. Even if you only ride once or twice a week, you can cut down on carbon emissions and get some exercise.

Optimize computer: A computer that is overloaded with unnecessary files or is not running well can use more power than one that is working properly.

Deleting old files that you don't need will make your computer work less to find the right file. Keeping a current virus protection program as well as maintaining regular disk defragmentation will keep the processor from needing to work harder. Keeping the vents cleaned out from dust will also make the computer not have to overwork to keep the unit cool. (Around The House)

Convert to PDF: If you work in an office that is constantly printing out forms or notices and passing them out to every employee, try making them PDF files instead and emailing them to the entire staff. Some forms that need to be filled out can be filled out online and even if they can't, each individual employee can decide if they need to print it out on their own. This way only the people who need a paper copy need to print it, and don't forget to show them how to print on both sides of the paper! (Around The House)

Switch to recycled paper products: Any office, no matter how computer savvy they are, still needs to use a fair amount of paper. Switching to recycled paper can help reduce the amount of trees used in your paper consumption. According the **University of Southern Indiana**, "Each ton (2000 pounds) of recycled paper can save 17 trees, 380 gallons of oil, three cubic yards of landfill space, 4000 kilowatts of energy, and 7000 gallons of water. This represents a 64% energy savings, a 58% water savings, and 60 pounds less of air pollution!" (Around The House)

Switch to recycled toner cartridges: When you do need to print or make copies (hopefully two sided on recycled paper), you will definitely need toner. You can recycle your empty toner cartridges and use remanufactured cartridges. According to **TonerRecycle.net**, there are 350 million toner cartridges placed in landfills all over the world every year. (Around The House)

Bring a lunch: For some people, the idea of getting up early to make a meal they aren't even going to eat for another 4 hours just seems like a chore. Why do that when you can easily go pick something up for lunch? Well, because you have to get in your car and drive to a restaurant or store and then drive back to work. There are exceptions to the rule. Maybe you have a cafe on the same block or a cafeteria in the building, but if you do drive to lunch every day, stop. I used to do this same thing and I have found that the 10 minutes it takes to make a lunch is well worth it. I get a more nutritious meal and I actually get to relax for my entire lunch break. Sometimes I will make my lunch the night before and just pop it in the fridge. Get a set of reusable containers to put your lunch components in so you don't need to use disposable plastic bags or tin foil.

Reuse packing materials: Start saving the packing materials that come in shipments to your office and reuse them to pack the shipments going out of your office. You wouldn't believe how many business throw packing materials away. Not only will you save a ton of room in the landfills, but you will also save money by not buying new packing material. I have a big bag of used packing material at my house which is more than enough, so now when we get new packing material we take it to the local pack and mail store for them to recycle. (Around The House)

Pack smarter: It never ceases to amaze me when I receive a package in the mail and the item is the size of a pack of gum but the box could easily hold a printer. Why send out that much cardboard and packing material for such a small item? Pack items in appropriately sized boxes and save a few trees and some packing material.

Sign up for file sharing: Instead of mailing documents, pictures or video through the mail to coworkers or colleagues, use a file sharing service. Services such as **Google Drive** or **Dropbox** are great for distributing information to a select group of people. You upload your documents, pictures or video to the service and you can either make it public or you can send the recipient a link that only they can use. They have free versions that work for smaller files but if you need more space, a paid account is fairly inexpensive. Another option if you work in a business that needs contracts signed regularly is a service like **Docusign**. This is a great option to get contracts signed fast and free of paper and postage.

Upgrade devices: Instead of buying brand new devices and scrapping the old ones, get repairs and upgrades. Now days it's not uncommon for a repair to cost enough to justify just buying a new device, but if the device needs minor repair or can be improved with an upgrade, that might give you a couple more years until needing to replace it. My last computer was getting old enough for me to start thinking about buying a new one, but after I spent $40 to double the RAM, it ran for another year before the video card burned out. That repair would have cost more than a new computer so I bought a reconditioned computer and donated the old computer to a computer shop so they could reuse the parts. Be resourceful and you'd be surprised how a small investment can get you a year or two of life out of a device. And when you do need to replace something, look into refurbished items (which I talk about more in the next chapter). (Around The House)

Use a smaller font: When you're working in an office environment and you might be printing a lot of documents, reducing the font can save you a page or two on longer documents. Of course you don't want to make it so small that it can't be read, but you can go from a 12 pt font to an 11 pt font and not notice much difference. Of course using PDFs through email is the greenest option, but if you do need to print out documents, use this trick so save a little paper and make sure you print on both sides of the paper.

Reuse file folders: Instead of throwing away file folders when you're done with the contents, put a label sticker over the tab and reuse it. I've noticed that this is pretty common already, but for anyone who doesn't already, reuse those file folders.

Switch to video conferencing: You'd be amazed at how much time and money large companies spend on travel expenses for meetings and conferences. Not only are they spending money, but they are burning fuel to get from point A to point B. These days, technology has provided us with so many alternatives to traveling for work. There are a wide variety of video conferencing options to make it quick and easy to meet with customers and colleagues on the other side of the world.

Remove disposable items: It's easy to just stock up the break room with paper cups, plastic spoons and paper plates, but is it really necessary? Putting a bunch of coffee cups in the break room and having each employee be responsible for washing and drying the cup at the end of the day might be a little more work, but any responsible adult should be able to handle it. Better yet, ask each employee bring in a mug to contribute to the break room. Then throw some cheap utensils and plates in a cupboard and you'll be surprised at how much less garbage there is in your break room trash can at the end of the day. (Around The House)

In The Car

Clean out your car. One of the easiest ways to increase your fuel efficiency is to reduce the weight of your vehicle. This can be done by cleaning out your car regularly. Having your trunk or back seat littered with clothes, shoes, books and other items just makes you burn more fuel. Keeping the exterior of your vehicle clean will also increase its aerodynamics which can also increase fuel efficiency. A clean, smooth surface has less wind resistance than a dirty surface.

Pay attention to your driving: The way you drive can greatly affect your fuel economy. If you floor the gas as soon as a stop light turns green and accelerate as quickly as possible, you will use more fuel than if you just gradually accelerate. If you are constantly gunning it, trying to weave through traffic, you will lower your fuel economy. Some ways to increase your fuel economy while you drive are to accelerate gradually, keep your speed down and shift earlier if you drive a manual transmission. Pay attention to your driving and you can spend less money at the pump. Paying attention to what's ahead will give you time to slow down gradually as well. If you are always slamming on your brakes every time you need to stop, you'll wear through brakes faster and need to change them out more often. Slowing more gradually will save material and waste in the long run.

Check fluids and tire pressure: Ensuring your car is full of fluids and air can increase your fuel economy and make your car last longer. When your tire pressure is low, your vehicle has to work harder to move, thus using more fuel in the process. It also wears your tires faster which will result in needing new tires more often. Checking the tire pressure every couple of weeks will keep the pressure correct which will save you gas and make your tires last longer. Making sure the fluids in your car are at the proper levels is just as important. When the engine is low on fluids, the engine has to work harder in order to move. This makes your fuel economy go down and makes your engine wear out faster. Always check the oil, transmission fluid, power steering fluid, brake fluid, coolant and air filter every couple of weeks to ensure your car is always working at maximum efficiency.

Use cruise control when you can: Cruise control is not just a handy feature to use while traveling long distances, it can also increase your fuel efficiency. Using the cruise control to regulate your speed over long distances will save fuel by eliminating the extra gas you will use speeding up and slowing down while trying to keep a constant speed on your own. A human is no match for a computer when it comes to keeping a consistent speed and that is the key to getting the best fuel economy you can.

Communication

Encourage family members: We all know those people who are constantly pushing everyone around them to believe in their cause. Don't be like that person. You can encourage your friends and family to follow green practices without being pushy. They may be using a disposable item without thinking about it, so you can let them know they should get a reusable option. Or better yet, get them one as a gift. Subtle reminders are a good way to go instead of being overly pushy.

Call or write to your representatives: The best way to make things change permanently is to change the laws to support those practices. Call or write to your local representatives to let them know you support green practices and regulations that may be on the books. Getting your local politicians involved in going green will help change the state of the environment for the future.

Report water issues: I can't count the amount of times I've been driving through town and saw a broken sprinkler head just gushing water out into a parking lot. In those instances, jot down the location so you can call your local water company and report the issue. If it's in an area that's controlled by the city, they can send a crew out to fix it. If the problem is on private property, they can investigate and make sure the property owner is aware of the issue.

GOING GREEN FOR NEXT TO NOTHING

Around The House

LED lighting: One of the best ways to save electricity is to swap your incandescent and even your compact fluorescent bulbs with LED bulbs. They use a fraction of the energy needed to power both the other light options. The best way to do it economically is to swap out the bulbs as they burn out. The LED bulbs are significantly more expensive, but they last far longer and use so much less electricity that you will instantly see the difference on your electricity bill. (At Work)

Install dimmer switches: Not all lights need to be full power all the time. Dimmer switches are an inexpensive way to be able to customize your lighting needs and save a little power in the process. Just make sure the LED bulbs you use in those lights are compatible with dimmer switches. (At Work)

Water conservation: On top of some of the free options mentioned in the 'Going Green Without Spending A Dime' section, you can also purchase new plumbing fixtures that are designed to save water. Shower heads and sink faucets used to commonly put out 2.5 GPM (gallons per minute). Newer, more water conscious fixtures put out as low as 1.2 GPM. Swapping out a shower head can be an inexpensive way to save water and save money on your water bill in the long run. Unless you buy a fancy shower head with massage settings and a Bluetooth speaker, your average shower head could pay for itself in less than a year.

Insulate your water heater: Your water heater is constantly working to keep the water inside it hot. If the temperature of the air on the outside of the water heater is cold, that will make the water inside the water heater cool faster which will cause the water heater to work harder to keep it at a high temperature. Use a water heater insulation kit on your water heater to help keep the hot water inside from cooling off as fast.

Recondition batteries / use rechargeables: Don't let all those disposable batteries go to the landfill, start using rechargeable batteries. Rechargeable AA and AAA batteries are pretty inexpensive and are great for all of your remote controls and small electronics that constantly need new batteries. You can also recondition batteries, especially car batteries. There are great instructions to recondition car batteries at **The Do-It-Yourself World**.

Use a programmable thermostat: Lowering your heat by three degrees is a great way to save energy while you are home, but why heat the house at all while you're away? You can get a programmable thermostat for your home pretty inexpensively. This way you can program the heat to turn off when you go to work and turn back on 30 minutes before you get home so it's a comfortable temperature when you walk through the door. You can also program it to turn the heat down at night while you're sleeping. The heat doesn't need to be as high when you are tucked in under a pile of blankets. (At Work)

Use cloth towels and napkins: Paper towels and napkins are disposable items that most people don't give a second thought about buying on a regular basis, but do you really need them? You can replace paper towels with cloth rags. As a bonus, you can upcycle your old t-shirts into rags to replace the disposable paper towels! Buying a couple sets of cloth napkins will cost some money up front, but will save you money in the long run since you won't be buying paper napkins any more. You'll also keep that waste out of the landfills.

Use power strips to turn off power draw: Wall chargers and small electronic can still draw power even if you aren't using them. An inexpensive powerstrip can be a convenient way to turn them all off at once. I plug all of my chargers into one powerstrip and then I can just flip one switch to cut power to all of them at once. When they aren't in use, I can easily make sure they aren't drawing any extra power. (At Work)

Add house plants: Plants are good for you and the environment. Not only do they produce oxygen, but they clean the air as they cycle carbon dioxide in and oxygen out. Pick plants that are low maintenance and are indigenous to your area and they will add color to your home while cleaning the air you breath. (At Work)

Use a French press and manual bean grinder: Not only does your drip coffee maker use energy to make your coffee, it's not the best way to make coffee. A French press is said to be the best way to make your coffee. Just heat a pot of water and the rest of the work is manual. And don't get me started with the new, on-demand, single cup coffee makers. They create so much waste just to have a single cup of coffee. You can also switch your electric grinder for a hand crank grinder. Save energy and burn a few calories at the same time.

Use eco friendly cleaning products: Just because a product is made for cleaning doesn't necessarily mean it's clean itself. Many cleaning products contain bleach, ammonia and other chemicals that are harmful to the environment. When you use these products and rinse the residue down the sink, It can be harmful to the environment around where your sewage ends up. Even if you have a septic tank, the bacteria in the tank that helps break down the contents could be reduced or killed off. That means your septic tank could fill faster and need to be pumped more often. Eco friendly cleaning products are safe for living organisms and break down without a negative impact on the environment. (At Work)

Switch to reusable menstrual products: There are many options these days for replacing disposable menstrual products such as tampons and maxi pads. A menstrual cup can be inserted during a woman's cycle and then dumped out into the toilet when needed. There are also options like cloth pads or specially designed panties that are meant to be worn during a woman's period and work just as effectively as disposable options. These items can save money and reduce waste.

Use cloth diapers: There is a myth that gets perpetuated by the environmental community that 90% of landfills are just disposable diapers. This myth is not even close to being true. The real number is more like 3% of landfills but that doesn't mean we should just keep using disposable diapers. If we could eliminate 3% of what goes into landfills, that would still be a huge victory. Using cloth diapers is one way we can do that. My wife and I used cloth diapers with both of our children and it was a great experience. There was the initial expense of buying the diapers, but then we never had to buy diapers again. Using them were just as easy as using disposables and even though there was the added work involved in cleaning them, it was not as labor intensive as some people think it will be. If you can't commit to using 100% cloth diapers, get a few to start with and use them whenever you get a chance.

Get books used instead of new: I know that a lot of people love the feel of a brand new book. The clean, crisp pages being turned for the first time is a great feeling. It's unnecessary though, and if you want to help cut down on waste, buying used books is a much better option. You can find almost anything you're looking for at a second hand book store or on Amazon. If you shop on Amazon, they always provide an option to buy it used from a number of available shops or individuals. Buy it used, read it and sell it back to the bookstore. The cycle continues.

Recycle / upcycle old items and clothes: Some old items can be upcycled at home with nothing but a pair of scissors. Sometimes you will need to buy some additional supplies to turn your old shirts into the new item you want. Even if you have to spend a few bucks on a zipper and some clasps, there's no reason not to turn your old worn out items into beautiful new ones.

Get eco friendly crayons for your kids: Every child loves to color. Most adults still love to color as well. Unfortunately, most mass produced crayons are made with paraffin wax which is derived from oil. The process of making crude oil into a crayon is a energy and pollution heavy process. A great alternative is to buy or make your kids crayons from beeswax or soy wax. You can find instructions for making your own crayons on the blog **Nourishing Joy**.

Replace electric kitchen gadgets with manual versions: I thought electric can openers were only in movies. I've seen countless scenes of movie characters opening a can of dog or cat food with an electric can opener, but can't think of a time when I've ever seen one in real life. Well, it turns out people do own and use them. Why? For $1.99 you can get a classic metal can opener. You know, the one with a bottle opener at the end of the handle. Not only does is save electricity, it easily opens a can 10 times faster than the bulky electric version. Plus it saves counter space. I don't know why they even still make electric can openers. Don't forget to replace your electric carving knife and your electric coffee grinder... Do you not have hands?

Keep your freezer full, it runs more efficiently: When you have an empty freezer, the cooling unit is working at its maximum to keep it cold. When you have your freezer packed to the gills, most of that frozen frozen food, helps keep the freezer cold. The insulation within the freezer keeps the frozen food from thawing and just like when you put a bunch of ice in a cooler and shut the lid, the frozen food actually helps cool the freezer, letting the cooling system take more breaks. Not only do you have more variety of delicious food, your electricity bill will go down. Make sure your freezer is full and rotate the stock so the food doesn't go to waste.

Ask power company about green energy: Some power companies have a department that specializes in renewable energy. If your power company has the option, you can call and request your electricity come from a renewable source. There are also third party companies who you can pay to increase renewable energy production on your behalf. It's confusing and it will actually end up costing you more, but it could give you some piece of mind in the long run. (At Work)

Caulk all the windows and doors: This is easily one of the first things anyone should do if they are trying to make their home more energy efficient. After that, the caulk should be checked every year. Ensure all weather striping in doors and windows is in proper working order as well. As a lifetime building contractor, I cannot tell you how many cold, drafty houses I have fixed with a few tubes of caulk and a door sweep.

Repair instead of replace: We live in a time when almost all products have become disposable. You can buy a Kindle Fire for $50 and if it breaks in a year, toss it and buy a new one. I don't know anyone who doesn't have a new phone every year as soon as they're able to upgrade. We've forgotten that things can be fixed. If you can get an item fixed for a reasonable price, why throw it away? This is especially true for larger items like appliances and tools. If you have a broken tool, you can go to **www.ereplacementparts.com**, buy the parts you need and fix them yourself. I've repaired many power tools in less than 30 minutes with $15 worth of parts. (At Work)

Buy refurbished instead of new: I had an eight year old iMac that was going to cost twice as much to fix than it was to replace. I replaced it with a refurbished Mac Mini and gave the iMac to the repair shop as many of the parts could still be used to repair other devices. People think that refurbished products are "used" products, but they aren't. Most refurbished products are actually brand new. They were purchased, had a factory defect and got returned to the store. The store then sends it back to the manufacturer where a technician goes through it and fixes the factory defect and checks over the rest of the product. A refurbished product is actually going to be better than it's "off the shelf" counterpart since it has actually been cleaned and tested by a real person. (At Work)

Buy quality products: A lot of consumer goods get a bad reputation these days for being cheaply made and unfortunately, it's true. We get mass produced goods, shipped over from China and they are only designed to appease our short attention span. Instead of ordering the cheapest product you can find on Amazon or Ebay, ensuring you will need to replace it within a year when it breaks, spend a little more on a quality product. You will spend less in the long run if you spend more now and you will throw less broken products in the trash. If you can, get something made locally, preferably by hand. Obviously, there isn't much you can do if you are purchasing an iPad or a PS4, but for items like furniture, appliances, tools and clothes, there is a definite gap between price and quality. (At Work)

Make sure your appliances are working properly: Getting your appliances repaired when broken and regularly serviced will ensure they stay working properly. When a machine has to work harder in order to do its job, it uses more power in the process.

Grow your own herbs: Setting up a herb garden at home is a great way to save money and have fresh herbs for cooking all the time. Any time you grow your own food you help the environment by cutting down on production and transportation of food.

Plant a tree: This shouldn't need an explanation but I'll give you one anyway. Tree are good for the environment. That's simple enough on its own, but if you plant a tree on your property, pick a location where the tree will shade your house. Save some money on cooling during the summer by using the tree to shade your house. You can also use the the tree to shade your AC unit. The unit will have to work less to create cold air which will save energy.

Invest in a zippo: If you smoke or use a lighter frequently, invest in a good zippo or other type of refillable lighter. Anything disposable is bad.

Upgrade your razor: Speaking of disposable items, razors are very commonly disposable, but they don't have to be. You can switch to a straight razor which never needs to be replaced. If that's a little too extreme for you, you can switch to a safety razor. They have a single, very thin blade that needs replacing. There is no plastic used in the production of safety razors. If you have a window in your bathroom, you can invest in a solar powered, electric shaver.

Switch answering machine to voicemail: The more electronic devices you have in your home, the more electricity you need to power them. If you still have an old answering machine in your home, swap it out for a voicemail service. You can get all your message from wherever you are and you can save a little electricity in the process. (At Work)

Switch to certified coffee: If you are a coffee drinker, don't just buy any coffee. Spend a little more on a certified coffee. There are multiple certifications for coffee and you can learn about them in the "Knowledge" section at the end of the book. Most of them have various requirements for the growers that greatly increase environmental friendliness. (At Work) (On The Go)

Convert toilet to dual flush: Most toilets use way more water than they need to in order to flush, especially if it's only flushing urine. Unfortunately, a lot of people aren't very happy with the performance of low flow toilets. Now you can get a dual flush toilet that allows you to choose between a full flush, for those heavy loads, or half flush, for all other times. You can save a lot of water by using the half flush and you will notice it on your water bill.

Replace furnace filter: Maintenance is clearly important when it comes to going green. When appliances work properly, they use less energy. Your furnace is no different. Getting your furnace serviced and replacing the filter will ensure your air stays clean and your furnace works efficiently.

Buy carbon credits: There is a lot of debate about carbon credits. I'm not going to get into the politics of carbon credits but I will list them as an option if they are something you feel might work for you. In my opinion, there is always something you can do to make your life a little greener, but if you feel like you have exhausted all of your option but still want to do more, looking into carbon credits may work for you.

On The Go

Reusable shopping bags: The plastic shopping bags you get from the grocery store have become a hot button issue in recent years. Some places have even gone so far as to make them illegal. Even if they are still legal in your area, they have a huge negative impact on the environment. From the space they take up in landfills to the oil it takes to produce them, plastic grocery bags are just bad news. The great news is that you can buy reusable shopping bags in all shapes and sizes. You can get them straight from the grocery store or you can buy custom bags with your favorite sports team logo on them. You can get insulated bags that will keep your cold item cold on the ride home. The options are plentiful and the bags are inexpensive.

Reusable produce bags: Not only can you replace the plastic shopping bags, you can also replace the smaller plastic bags that you find in the produce section. You can buy smaller mesh bags to use for your fruits and vegetables during your shopping trip. These are not sold in as many places as the shopping bags, but you can find many different sizes and types online.

Use your own coffee cup at the cafe: Many people don't realize that you can bring your own cup to nearly any cafe and they will be more than happy to use it instead of a disposable option. Bring your favorite mug or if you are on the go, pick up a travel mug and have them make your coffee in that. Some coffee shops have travel mugs you can purchase and any time you use it you get a discount. Check with your favorite cafe and see what they have to offer.

Use a reusable water bottle: If you're like me, you love to have ice cold water to drink wherever you are. I used to be guilty of buying countless bottles of water at convenience stores, two, sometimes three times a day. Of course those bottles would go into the recycle bin, but why even create that waste. Investing in a good reusable water bottle that you can refill and take with you. I got two. I keep one in the fridge at my office and one with me. I swap them out whenever I need to during the day. My job keeps me coming and going to and from my office throughout the day. I also like my water ice cold and you're like me, you can buy reusable bottles that have an ice insert that you can freeze before use to keep your water cold during your activities. (At Work)

At Work

Use a reusable lunchbox or bag: Instead of bringing your lunch in a paper bag or styrofoam container, get a reusable lunch box or bag. Not only will you save money and waste in the long run, but you can get a lunch container that is insulated so your lunch stays cold longer. Or you can get a thermos and have hot soup for lunch on a cold day. Not only save waste but have comfort food for lunch.

Motion sensing switches: At the office, you will probably need the lights on all day so your employees or coworkers can see what they are doing. Some areas don't apply though. Storage rooms and bathrooms are great examples of areas where the lights get left on all day but the rooms aren't occupied very often. A motion sensing switch will make the lights automatically turn on when someone enters the room and then automatically turns them off when it senses no motion for a certain amount of time. (Around The House)

In The Car

Keep up to date on vehicle maintenance: Keeping your car clean and checking fluids will save you money and energy in the long run, but you should also make sure you keep the engine tuned up and the filters clean. Having your car regularly serviced will not only help your vehicle perform at peak efficiency, saving on carbon emissions, but will also save you money and increase the life of your car. Bankrate has a great article on the **True Cost of Not Maintaining Your Car**.

Use a car wash: The problem with washing your car at home, in your driveway, is that the waste water runs down into the storm drain. Unlike your sewer drain in your house that goes to a water treatment plant before it gets discharge into the environment, the storm sewer goes right into rivers and streams. So all of the oil and gas residue on your car along with the cleaning agent gets washed straight into the environment. Car wash stations are regulated to treat the rinse water before discharging it. They may also treat and reuse some of the rinse water as well as reducing the amount of water that comes out of the high pressure nozzle. You don't actually need that much water to create a high pressure stream.

Use a waterless or rinseless car wash: If you only build up a minimal amount of surface dirt on your vehicle or have just a dirty spot on it, you can use a waterless car wash system. It is a spray can of detergent that you spray on the dirty spot and then wipe clean with a rag. If your vehicle is a little dirtier and you need to clean the entire thing, you can go with a rinseless car wash system. This is a special cleaner you mix in with a bucket of water. You wash your vehicle with that and then use a clean cloth to dry it off and your car is clean with minimal water usage.

GOING GREEN WITHIN A MODERATE PRICE RANGE

Around The House

LED lighting: If you want to upgrade the lighting in your home faster than replacing bulbs as they burn out, you can replace all the bulbs in your house with LED bulbs all at once. That could cost you a few hundred dollars depending on the type of bulbs that are in your house. Standard bulbs have become fairly inexpensive, but if you have the small halogen lights that are common in kitchen and bath lights, the LED version can be a bit on the pricey side. (At Work)

High end programmable thermostat: You can save quite a bit of energy by lowering your thermostat by just 3 degrees. You can save even more energy by lowering it when you go to bed and when nobody will be home. A programmable, digital thermostat is a great option to make sure your home is only being heated when it needs to be. They now have what are referred to as "learning thermostats" which will automatically learn your habits and use your heating and cooling in the most efficient way possible. (At Work)

Start a compost pile: Some major cities like Seattle, have pretty good composting programs, but if you would like to compost on your own, it's a great way to cut down on waste. You can purchase a large bin that is designed specifically for composting. The compost makes great natural fertilizer for your garden.

Add plants that don't need watering: If you are going to add a few plants around your property, make sure you use plants that are indigenous to your area and can survive in your climate without extra watering. You can also just go with plants that are used to getting low levels of water like cactus, bromeliads and succulents.

Get an energy audit: **An energy audit** is where a professional comes into your house and usually sets up a device in your doorway that blows air through your house and identifies how airtight your home is. The more airtight your home is the better as this means your heating and cooling efforts are getting maximum effect. It can tell you that you need to go around and caulk doors and windows and add door sweeps to close up gaps. They will also check your heating ducts for openings that might need to be repaired. They can identify ways that you can lower your home's energy consumption.

Use a rain collection barrel: It's amazing that we have free water that falls right from the sky in most areas of the world and so many of us don't ever use it. If you do have a flower bed or a garden that needs regular watering, why not use a rain collection barrel? You can put a barrel at the bottom of your home's downspout and, depending on your local rainfall, store enough water to never have to turn on a hose to water your flowers and garden. Check your local ordinances because some cities have sadly made collecting water on your own property illegal. Fortunately, there has been a recent trend of those ordinances getting lifted.

Cover your pool: If you have a pool, there is a simple way to make that pool a little greener. Cover it when it's not in use. This will not only keep the pool cleaner, but it will make the water evaporate more slowly, making you need to fill it less often. This also applies to hot tubs but those are much more common to have covers already.

Clean heater ducts: We keep coming back to maintenance as a way to keep your house as green as possible. Cleaning your heater ducts is an important part of that. Now, you can take a shop vac and periodically shove it into your vents to suck out any dust and debris, but you won't be able to reach every part of your heat duct system. At some point you will need to have a professional come out with a special vacuum to completely clean out the ducts in your home. Once this is done the air will flow through them much more efficiently, causing your furnace to do less work in order to heat your house.

Replace toilets with low flow: There is a cheaper option of converting your current toilet to a dual flush toilet, but sometimes those kits don't work perfectly. You can replace your entire toilet with a dual flush or just a low flow toilet in general. This will reduce the amount of gallons of water your toilet uses with each flush and will add up to great savings over time. Remember, if you are going to replace a toilet, and the old one still works, donate it to a reuse company like the **Habitat For Humanity ReStore**.

Install ceiling fans: If you are using air conditioning as means of cooling off your house, a lot of time you can get the same effect by using a ceiling fan. If you don't have a ceiling fan, you can have one installed for a moderate cost. If you have a light fixture in the center of the room, you can just purchase a ceiling fan and have it installed where the light is. If you don't, then you will need to hire an electrician to wire it up and add a switch for it on the wall. The cost of that will easily pay for itself if you can stop using your AC for minor cooling needs.

Add storm windows: Do you have old single pane windows but don't have the money to replace your windows? You can add storm windows over your existing windows to get additional protection from air leakage and heat loss. They make interior and exterior storm windows. Interior storm windows are easier to install and maintain since they are not outside exposed to the elements.

Install curtains drapes and blinds: Adding curtains or blinds to your windows, especially to the windows that face the sun during the day, can block the sunlight and keep the inside of your house cooler. The **United States Department of Energy** states that light colored curtains can reduce heat gain by 33% and blinds can reduce heat gain by 45%. Using drapes or curtains over windows in the winter can add an extra layer of insulation to keep heat in. Just keep in mind that you might earn more heat from the sun if you open the curtains during the day. Do a little experimenting to find out the best configuration of blinds and curtains. (At Work)

Add an awning over windows: Awnings over windows can shade the window from the sun. This can reduce the amount of heat coming into your home during the summer. It's a good idea to add a retractable awning so you can pull it back and take advantage of the sunlight in the winter.

Get electric lawn tools: The options for electric and even cordless lawn maintenance tools has blown up in the last few years. You can get cordless electric lawn mowers, weed eaters and even chainsaws. I use a corded electric lawn mower which cuts the grass just fine as long as I don't let it get too long. I also have a cordless weed eater that has two batteries and I can get all my weed eating done with just those two batteries. I charge them and have them ready for the next use. When you have rechargeable batteries, don't forget to unplug them when they are done charging as they will continue to draw power while they are plugged in.

Use convection heating: If you have standard electric heating, just having hot air blown out of a single location is not the most efficient means of heating a room. A convection heater mounts to a wall blowing hot air up and sucking cold air from the bottom. This creates a circulation of hot air that will keep the room a few degrees warmer all the time. It's not a heater that turns on and off as the room needs heat. It uses a small amount of energy to always raise the room temperature a few degrees making that one room that's always a little chilly, just a bit warmer and more comfortable.

On The Go

Get your car a tune up: Getting a full tune up for your car is a simple way to keep your car running at its most efficient. A tune up generally replaces old dirty small parts that aren't working at their top performance. It also includes making adjustments needed to keep you car working properly. When your engine is clean and working properly it uses the least amount of energy to push you forward.

Install a MPG meter: A Miles-Per-Gallon meter plugs into your engine and gives you a display that lets you know the real time MPG you are getting as you drive. Some newer vehicles already have these built into their dash and if you have one, you should start using it. When you have one of these you can see how your driving affects your fuel efficiency as you drive. This can let you know how to adjust your driving habits to use these fuel and increase your MPG.

Add a drive analyzer: There are a few types of devices that you plug into your vehicle that will analyze your driving and send suggestion of how to get better fuel efficiency to your smart phone. The two common devices ar **Automatic** and **Zubie**. You need to have a car that is no older than 1996. That is when they started putting the data port in vehicles so drivers could add devices to their vehicles.

At Work

Bike to work: This is one of the options in the "Going Green Without Spending A Dime" section. That option is free if you already own a bike and gear. If you don't, you will need to buy a bike, a helmet, lights, a reflective vest and any other items you might need to ride safely to work. A good bicycle can cost in the hundreds to thousands of dollars. But you can make all that money back by not buying gas, needing car insurance and auto maintenance costs.

GOING GREEN WITH A PRICETAG

Around The House

Add insulation to your home: There is no better way to increase the efficiency of your home than by adding insulation where needed. This isn't going to apply to newer homes, but in areas where homes are 20 years old or more, most of them will be seriously lacking on insulation. You can have insulation blown into the attic space. This will keep the heat from traveling up and out of your ceiling. You can also have holes drilled into the exterior walls of your house and have insulation blown into them as well. That will take a professional to come in and patch the holes. This will greatly reduce the amount of heat you need in your home, saving a ton of energy and money.

Upgrade to high efficiency appliances: If you have older appliances, chances are their efficiency is on the low end. You can install new appliances that are high efficiency and make all that money back on your energy bill. You can get high efficiency versions of refrigerators, ovens, stoves, dishwashers, clothes washers and dryers, hot water heaters and furnaces. If you were to replace all of these at once, you would see your home energy consumption drop like a brick.

Remodel the kitchen to place the appliances better: If you are going to replace your appliances for high efficiency versions, you could just take it up another level and remodel your kitchen to be a more efficient layout. If your refrigerator gets hit with sunlight for the better part of the day or sits right next to the oven which gets frequent use, you might be causing your fridge to work hard. That sunlight is going to warm up the refrigerator from the outside while it struggles to keep the food cold inside. You can move the appliances to places that work better for your cooking needs and to keep them working more efficiently.

Replace Windows: Do you have old single pane windows? It might be time to upgrade to new high efficiency windows. Going from single pane to double pane windows can increase your home's efficiency by 18-24% according to **Home Advisor**. There are many additional technologies that can be added to the windows that can get you up to a 30-50% increase in home efficiency. Not only will you save money and use less energy, double pane windows will reduce exterior noise and give you a quieter home.

Upgrade landscaping to plants that don't need watering: Having a giant yard of green grass is not very environmentally friendly. Keeping grass mowed and green takes a lot of water and energy. Upgrading your home's landscaping to replace grass with low maintenance plants that don't need to be watered will save a ton of resources and will save a ton of your time. Not having to spend all of your free time mowing, weed eating and watering your yard will allow you to spend your time relaxing.

Move to a more efficient house: If your current home is just a mess of energy inefficiency and it will take too much to upgrade, consider moving into a house that works better for you. Maybe you can move to a home that is closer to your office, allowing you to bike or even walk to work. Maybe you can downsize your home and spend less on heating and cooling costs. Maybe you can find a house that has a smaller yard that needs less maintenance, has more efficient appliances, or a combination of any of these. No matter what your needs are, there may be a house out there that meets your needs better than your current house.

Install a new roof: Most residential roofs are either cedar shake, clay tile or asphalt shingles. These days, asphalt shingles are by far the most common type of roofing. The most common color is black or a shade of dark gray just a little lighter than black. According to the **United States Department of Energy**, a dark colored roof can get up to 150 degrees. A light colored roof can stay up to 50 degrees cooler which will keep your home cooler and need less energy to keep cool in the summer. I understand that a white roof doesn't always work on a lot of houses, but even a lighter gray can vastly improve the energy efficiency of your home.

Install geothermal heating: A geothermal heating system uses a water pipe that travels deep into the earth and then comes back up, delivering hot water into the system. The temperature in the earth is much more constant than temperatures outside. The geothermal system takes advantage of the earth's natural heat in order to heat your home. It only uses a tiny bit of electricity to move the water in the system. They can be expensive to install but federal and local incentives can make up anywhere from 30-60% of the total cost of the system.

Install a tankless water heater: Most of the day, your hot water heater is just sitting there, keeping water hot, even when you aren't using it. According to **Consumer Reports**, heating water can account for 30% of your total home energy consumption. Replacing a gas water heater with a gas tankless water heater can save 22% of the energy used by a traditional water heater. Tankless water heaters can be a bit pricier than the traditional models, but if you are looking for energy conservation, they are definitely worth it.

Install solar panels: One of the best ways to decrease the carbon footprint of your home is to install solar panels. There are a ton of things to consider when thinking about adding solar panels to your home. The **United States Department of Energy** has a bunch of articles on the subject and I suggest starting there. Depending on your location and the amount of unobstructed sunlight hours you get per day you can potentially power your entire house with solar panels. Dropping your energy usage from electricity down to zero. (At Work)

Install a wind turbine: If you don't get a great amount of sunlight but have a decent amount of wind, you can install a wind turbine on your property. You can put it on a pole in your yard or you can put it on the peak of your roof. You can buy a pre-made turbine designed to hook right into your house or you can build one yourself. A wind turbine isn't going to produce as much electricity as solar panels will and unless you want your house covered in turbines, you probably won't be able to power your entire house on wind, but you will be able to drastically cut down on your dependency of the power company. (At Work)

On The Go

Replace car with more fuel efficient, hybrid or electric model: Some people drive a big truck or van and they need to due to their work, but if you have the option of replacing you larger, fuel guzzling vehicle, you should. Even if you only get a fuel efficient sedan to replace your SUV, you're going to save money and reduce your carbon footprint. You can go even further and get a hybrid or even an electric vehicle. If you only travel small distances to work or for errands, an all electric vehicle could work perfectly for you. If you still need some extra room but want to increase your fuel efficiency, a hybrid SUV might be a good option for you. They don't get the highest MPG, but they are better than regular gas SUVs. Every little bit helps. If you aren't sure which vehicle is best for you, check out **Fuel Efficiency's Most and Least Fuel Efficient Vehicles of 2016**.

At Work

Move your office to a more efficient building: If you own or are in charge of your business, it might work out better for you to move your office to a building with a higher commitment to environmental friendliness. A lot of office buildings are filled with old, energy guzzling lighting and haven't kept up on maintenance that would keep the building efficient. Most cities have buildings that focus on energy efficiency and if you are lucky, you might live in Seattle, San Francisco, Taipei, or Skanska, which are home to some of the greenest office building in the world. If you need an example, **The Bullitt Center** in Seattle is touted as the greenest office building in the world.

KNOWLEDGE

Coffee Certifications

Organic: Most people understand what organic means, but in case you don't, in order to be certified organic the crop must be grown without the use of most synthetic pesticides, herbicides and fertilizers.

Fair Trade Certified: Coffee and Tea can both be certified as Fair Trade. It started as a way to ensure the producers and workers were fairly compensated for their products. Producers are also required to meet criteria that include sustainable practices and labor standards.

Rainforest Alliance Certified: The rainforest alliance is another certification that help to keep rainforests safe from clearcutting. In order to have this certification the growers must meet a number of ecological requirements as well as fair treatment of workers.

Shade Grown certified: Which is also called "bird friendly coffee". The certification process ensures that there is enough canopy coverage where the coffee is grown. This is in response to the massive clearcutting that happens in the coffee farming industry and focuses on maintaining bird habitats. The certification also requires the coffee to be organic.

UTZ Certified: In order to get this certification, they must maintain transparency and traceability in their supply chain and use efficient farm management. This involves soil erosion prevention, minimizing water use and pollution, responsible use of chemicals, and habitat protection.

Places to Donate/Recycle
Goodwill: They take all clothes, furniture, electronics and household items. Some are even a recycling drop-off location for old televisions.

St. Vincent DePaul: This is like Goodwill. They take donations of all usable clothes and household items. You can even donate a car.

Salvation Army: Another place to donate general goods. They take all the same items as the other two and also take cars.

Habitat For Humanity: This organization does great work building housing for the needy. You can donate used building materials that are still in working order. They will either use the material in the construction of homes or sell it at one of their sales outlets to raise money for their cause.

Toner Cartridges: Nearly all of your local office supply store will take your old toner and ink cartridges and get them to the proper recycling facility.

Electronics: **The National Center for Electronic Recycling** is a great place to find information about electronics recycling in your local area. You can also visit your local electronics store and ask them where to drop of your old electronics.

Packing Material: Packing materials such as styrofoam peanuts are commonly accepted at local packing and mailing stores. If you bring them clean, usable packing material, they will accept it and use it in their business.

Junk Mail Opt-Out

OptoutPresceen: This site will allow you to opt-out of "pre-approved" credit card offers.

DMAChoice: This site allows you to opt-out of commercial junk mail such as coupons and advertisements.

GLOSSARY

BCE: Before Common Era.

CE: Common Era.

CFL: Compact Fluorescent Light.

Carpool: To drive a vehicle with more than one person to minimize the number of cars on the road.

Compost: Decayed organic material used as a plant fertilizer.

Disk Defragmentation: A Microsoft Windows utility that rearranges files on a disk to make them more easily located.

Electricity: A form of energy resulting from the existence of charged particles (such as electrons or protons), either statically as an accumulation of charge or dynamically as a current.

Energy: Power derived from the utilization of physical or chemical resources, especially to provide light and heat or to work machines.

Energy Audit: An assessment of the energy needs and efficiency of a building or buildings.

File Sharing: The practice of or ability to transmit files from one computer to another over a network or the Internet.

GPM: Gallons Per Minute. The amount of water that is allowed through faucet.

Going Green: Making more environmentally friendly decisions as to *reduce, reuse and recycle.*

Greenhouse Gases: A gas that contributes to the greenhouse effect by absorbing infrared radiation, e.g., carbon dioxide and chlorofluorocarbons.

LED: Light Emitting Diode.

Landfill: A place to dispose of refuse and other waste material by burying it and covering it over with soil, especially as a method of filling in or extending usable land.

MPG: Miles Per Gallon.

PDF: Portable Document Format.

pH: Is a measure of how acidic/basic water is. The range goes from 0 - 14, with 7 being neutral.

Recycle: Convert waste into reusable material.

Refurbished: Taking a non working device and repairing or cleaning it so it is in near-new condition.

Sustainable: (Sustainability) Able to be maintained at a certain rate or level.

Telecommute: To work from home, making use of the Internet, e-mail, and the telephone.

Thermostat: A device that automatically regulates temperature, or that activates a device when the temperature reaches a certain point.

Treehugger: Someone who protests to protect the environment. Named after 363 Hindu that were killed while hugging trees in protest of their harvest.

Upcycle: Reuse (discarded objects or material) in such a way as to create a product of a higher quality or value than the original.

Vampire Power: The electric power consumed by electronic and electrical appliances while they are switched off or in a standby mode.

Video Conference: A conference in which participants in different locations are able to communicate with each other in sound and vision.

Thanks for reading my book **GOING GREEN**
If you enjoyed it, please take the time to review it.

Also, check out my other book
DEFENDING YOUR CASTLE: A Guide To Home Security

Available as a Kindle E-Book on Amazon.com